NOTES ABOVE WATER

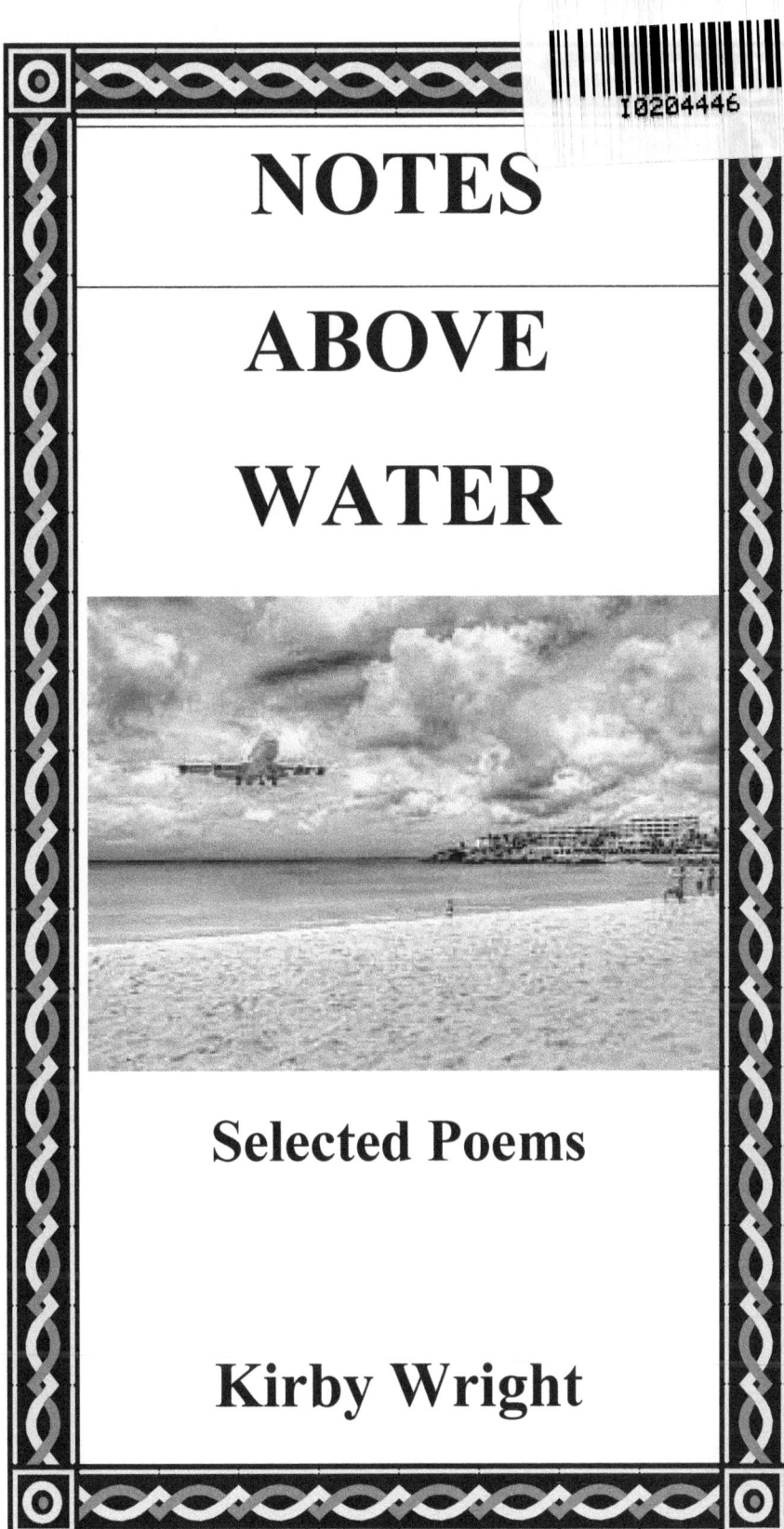

Selected Poems

Kirby Wright

Copyright © 2014 Kirby Wright

All rights reserved.

ISBN: 097410678X
ISBN-13: 978-0974106786

Published by Lemon Shark Press
San Diego, California
www.lemonsharkpress.com
ISBN: 097410678X
ISBN-13: 978-0974106786
Copyright © 2014 by Kirby Wright
All Rights Reserved

Publisher's Note
This is a work of poetic fiction. Names, characters, places,
and incidents either are the product of the author's imagination or are
used fictitiously, and any resemblance to actual persons, living or
dead, events, or locales is entirely coincidental.

Without limiting the rights under copyright reserved above, no part
of this publication may be reproduced, stored in or introduced into a
retrieval system, or transmitted in any form or by any means
(electronic, mechanical, photocopying, recording or otherwise),
without the prior written permission of both the copyright owner and
the above publisher of this book.

LEMON SHARK
PRESS

KIRBY WRIGHT

In memory of Dadio and June Spoon

ACKNOWLEDGEMENTS

I wish to thank the editors and staff of the following publications in which some of these poems first appeared or are forthcoming: *actual paper, Architrave Press, The Blinking Anthology, The Blue Moon Literary & Art Review, Brickplight, The Broadkill Review, Crab Fat Literary Magazine, Dead Flowers, The Doctor T. J. Eckleburg Review, Emerge Literary Journal, Empty Mirror, The Fiddleback, FishFood & LavaJuice, Foliate Oak Literary Magazine, Four Ties Lit Review, Gambling the Aisle, Gargoyle, Gravel, Line Zero, Marco Polo Arts Mag, Mascara Literary Review, Mason's Road, Meat For Tea: The Valley Review, Meat Whistle Quarterly, The Medulla Review, Owen Wister Review, Phantom Kangaroo, Poetic Diversity, Poetry Quarterly, Poetry South, Printer's Devil Review, The Prose-Poem Project, Red Booth Review, Santa Fe Literary Review, Sheepshead Review, SHOUT OUT UK, Star 82 Review, Tributaries, Tryst, The Voices Project, Wilderness House Literary Review* and *Writer's Bloc.*

Poems from this collection appeared in the chapbook *PERMANENT DAMAGE*, published by The Last Automat Press in 2013. Architrave Press published "Outside the Hotel" as a flash card/broadside in a limited edition on an antique letterpress in 2013 (Edition 4, Poem #7). "Sound Effects in Vista" won The Political Poet Poetry Competition in 2011.

CONTENTS

Book 1: CIRCLING FOR THE KILL

Permanent Damage	2
Summer Town	4
Once Immortal	5
At Fat Albert's, Sellwood	7
Sound Effects in Vista	9
Outside the Hotel	11
Self-Portrait while Shaving	12
Sea Cliff Man	15
Sounds from the Burbs	17
The Skulls	19
Bait	21
Incarceration	22
Memorial Notes	23
The Unattached	24

Book 2: FORCES OF NATURE

At Crater Lake, Oregon	27
The Great Oak	29
Sirens in Santa Cruz	30
Voice	32
SoCal Storm	33
Poolside at the Santa Fe Hilton	36
At the Coffee House	39
View from the 5th Floor	40
Message from a Vet	42
Notes from Crater Lake	44
Moon	46
30 Years Between Letters	48
Lost Love Revisited	50
The Last Aztec Mocha	51

Book 3: UNHOLY UNIONS

Marriage	53
Snacking with Mahmoud	55
Recluse	56
Barren	58
Confessions of a Retiree at Christmas	60
Night Marchers	62
To a Friend at the Ben Hur Apartments	63
Oceanside Beach	64
Poem for a Poet	67
Oceanfront Condo	69
Disney Postcard at Christmas	71
At Buccaneer Park	72
Leg of Jen	74
Son of Crab	76

Book 4: FINAL ACT IN PARIS

Outside the Boulangerie	78
Trip and Fall	81
Ring Finger	83
5 a.m. on a Work Day	84
The Secret World of Men	86
At Lofty Coffee, Encinitas	88
Moon River Interlude	90
Laws of Attraction	92
The Pain-Body	93
Pain Pills	94
Butchering Day	96
Keeping the Darkness Out	98
Ice Mother	100
Carrots on Snow	102
Final Act in Paris	103

Book 5: NOTES ABOVE WATER

Life Extension	106
Friedrich Speaks	109
View from the Burbs	111
Requiem for a Pool Man	113
The Young Novelist from Manila	115
The Monster in the House	122
On Finding a Lost Friend	124
The Girl With the Green Violin	125
Advice for a Poet Abroad	128
Trump Tower Waikiki	130
House With Dragon Trees	132
The Woman in the Black One Piece	133
The Neighbors	135
Notes Above Water	137

NOTES ABOVE WATER

for Darcy

Book 1
Circling
For
the Kill

Permanent Damage

They're outside driving in circles.

They want me to join them.

Circling makes me dizzy and forgetful.

I will become a poet, live on cupcakes and hope.

They want me to join them.

I can write about broken things and us.

I will become a poet, live on cupcakes and hope.

Permanent damage attracts me.

I can write about broken things and us.

The paper ignites, burning my words.

Permanent damage attracts me.

My pulse wears thin.

Cake bakes in the kitchen.

Circling makes me dizzy and forgetful.

The heart owns a limited number of beats.

They're outside driving in circles.

Summer Town

MY STREET? Strip of yellow lawns, oil-stained driveways, For Sale signs. A girl without eyes stares out the neighboring window. Asphalt shatters the cul-de-sac. Women push strollers past a popped beach ball skinning the gutter blue.

I'm knotted in apron frosting a cake. The room for entertaining fills with strangers. Most seem older. I recall photo albums stacked in the garage beside the bag of charcoal. When I was young I was way above average. Grandpa toasts—wine glasses rise. Who are these people? Outside, sun scorches the drive.

Once Immortal

Enough future for us both.

You could see it looking east.

Here, take my body.

I bloom with memories of you.

You could see it looking east.

Remember undressing in mirrors.

I bloom with memories of you.

Your teeth white as pearls.

Remember undressing in mirrors.

I collect water from the roof for tea.

Your teeth white as pearls.

Drinking rain slows the hours.

Consider the tragedy of pouring.

Here, take my body.

My best years are behind me.

Enough future for us both.

At Fat Albert's, Sellwood

HAPPY BIRTHDAY, DADIO. I'm playing counter boy in memory of you at this greasy spoon. I squeak on my vinyl stool and toy with a paper napkin. I try folding it into an angel. You'd tell me to act my age. My counter mates? A model-thin blonde in a Reed College sweatshirt and a bald man thumbing *The Oregonian*. The stink of fried eggs makes me nauseous. The waitress slides over a menu—she's doubling as the cook. I contemplate specials as steam fogs my cup.

Moments of indecision always summon you. "Learn to be decisive," you barked. I was your thorn, a chronic pain infected by the disgust of never making you proud. "Worthless," you mumbled one New Year's Eve. I learned defeat in our closed-door sessions, when screams and *I'm-sorry-Daddy's* joined the beat of the belt. I touched my wall and felt sorrow moving in waves through the redwood.

I vow to quit remembering. Memories send me beyond blue, into the indigo sky before twilight. Dadio, you carried hate into the hospital bed, where I spoon-fed you vanilla pudding and rubbed your feet under the sheets. Cold feet, I thought, icy heart. A nurse checked your pulse. "No more flowers," you scolded when my Christmas anthuriums arrived. I swore you'd never die but, if you did, I'd lug you like an overstuffed suitcase into the future.

A coffee refill comes—steam rises like a ghost. The blonde leaves and I crumple the angel napkin. The bald man retreats to the restroom. I feel as if I'm not human at all but a cold-blooded creature propped on a stool. The truth? Dadio, I've been shaped by you, folded by a lifetime of disappointment into a wrinkled toad.

Sound Effects in Vista

Boom-ah-boom-ah-boom-boom.

The walls and tables quiver.

The F-18s are at it again,

Practice bombing the Whiskey

And Zulu regions of neighboring

Pendleton. They carpet bomb

While I'm stretched on the carpet.

Fluffy folds her ears, scrambles

For cover. They bomb through

Letterman's monologue—I pretend

The jerk next door's banging his drums.

The windows rattle like hippie

Tambourines. Newborn hawks

Scream at the planets and stars.

Outside the Hotel

In the end

It's always tragedy.

We're haunted by loss

Or the hope

Of something to happen

That never will.

But our twilight dance

On the blue lawn

Outside the hotel

Means everything

In those hours of promise

Before the sun.

Self-Portrait While Shaving

Funny how cheeks

Fold in on themselves—

Creased leather

That will soon

Bubble and burn

In Joe's Crematorium.

Muscles?

I still have muscles.

Sometimes women

Mention my calves

If I wear shorts.

My scent reminds me

Of my old man.

My stink defeats

Tea tree roll-on.

Did Dadio hate me

For smelling young?

I skate razor

Over pockmarked visage

Trying to erase

Salt and pepper shadow.

Eyes wet, bloodshot.

Puckered lips

Webbed with wrinkles.

Blade nicks throat.

Blood resembles chocolate

Given the chance

To dry.

Smile.

Do a fake smile:

Teeth ash

From grinding meat,

Sucking marrow from bone.

Sea Cliff Man

Voilà the leaping spot in Del Mar.

Surfboards bob the indigo sea.

Super 8 threads through me.

We rode the Octopus at the fair.

Surfboards bob the indigo sea.

A girl in sapphire smiles.

We rode the Octopus at the fair.

Smells of cotton candy, donuts, vomit.

A girl in sapphire smiles.

You said I was invisible.

Smells of cotton candy, donuts, vomit.

My skin translucent as a ghost.

Listen to the gulls cry.

Super 8 threads through me.

Indian summer colds.

Voilà the leaping spot in Del Mar.

Sounds from the Burbs

Shoes echo on sidewalk:

Stroll, rush-walk and jog.

Car doors open, slam like bank vaults.

Trucks grumble in baritone.

Baby's cry transforms to giggle.

Skateboard wheels grind the asphalt.

"Eileen," a man calls, "Eileen!"

A fountain bubbles.

Song on the wind—

Is that "Joy to the World?"

Dog on the hill

Sings iambic pentameter.

The Skulls

There are these skulls

with necks and

bodies attached

rushing all over town

pretending they're immortal.

I see them

pulling skull dogs and

pushing skull babies

down the block.

Many drive cars.

Hey, Skullface,

The Day of the Coffin

draws near—

slow the hell down!

I see them

craning their necks

in grocery store lines,

sucking tabloids

through cavernous eyes.

They want the skull gods

to make mistakes

like them,

to taste the taste

of fading blood,

if only for a moment.

Bait

THE FIRE DIES. I throw in a chair with lion head arms for warmth. The feet extend back into my bedroom, claws scratching stone.

My room has a sliding glass door. Students slide it open, stroll past my bed, and leave through an oak door. I am the campus shortcut. A coed wearing a mini and platinum bouffant enters. She locks the glass and takes off her bouffant. She's bald. "I'm Bait," she goes, unbuckling her skirt. She tears off strips that were eyebrows. "Velcro," she admits.

We listen to the chair howl. Bait moves against me—I want to resist, yet can't. I feel as if I'm cheating on a lover. "Eat," she instructs. "Eat like a shark." Bait forces me to do things I ordinarily would not do. Soon I learn the taste of her salt.

Incarceration

I DRIVE BY where they hold you. Your campus resembles a business park—concrete cubes sporting thin vertical windows. Glass ink black, yet I can see my car passing through. You're tucked in the Theo Lacy wing. Grounds boast resort-green lawns, eucalyptus, roses in raised beds.

Across the street, the ash trees bend. Hydrants are milky-white. Chain-wire fences enclose a field with blue end zones. Goal posts the color of hydrants. Remember your touchdown in the big game? The cheerleaders loved you.

I hang a left and head back to the freeway. Clouds kill the sun. Shadows roll over the forgotten and tumble into the sea.

Memorial Notes

A NAKED BABY tickled on a bearskin rug. Fireplace crack-crackles. What is warm depends on moments. Snap pix of young evaporating. Laugh, cry, revel in haunted moments. Saw notches in oak counting the dead. Smell leaves turning ruddy orange. Friends are easy enemies. Lovers fade to ghosts. A man strolls the shore beneath tangled peaks, a lab leading him over ice. A baby's cry echoes the water.

The Unattached

A baby's cry rattles

Awake the unattached

On a Sunday morning,

Complicating hangovers

And assorted aches

With regret and self-loathing.

Why, what's wrong

With marriage?

Desperation sweeps the plains,

Sparked by the desire

To birth imagined children

And orchestrate picnics

Beside the diamond river.

Symphonies of calls and texts

Haunt the airwaves.

Legions of the single

Seek and surrender to partners

That might

Resemble their parents

In a score of minor ways.

Book 2

Forces

of

Nature

At Crater Lake, Oregon

This blue is beyond cobalt,

the color of Earth's oceans

viewed from Mars.

Dip your wine glass

into the lake.

Sip the melt.

No rivers in.

No rivers out.

Whatever arrives stays.

What mysterious currents

send *Llao's Fingers*

west from eastern shore?

Pines root the cliffs.

Trout rise to taste

volcanic dust.

White pelicans claim

the emerald pool

on Wizard Island.

Break off

a sprig of hemlock.

Open the soft needles.

Smell a hundred centuries

as the branches sway,

revealing the moon.

Llao's Fingers: patterns on the surface caused by the spirit of the slain god of the lake

The Great Oak

IT WAS A SCORCHING summer and the great oak was dying. Ferns drowned in a cascade of leaves. Frogs fled. Birds didn't land on the bare branches. A boy tied a leaf to a pole and held it up to shade a bough. 'It's the least I can do," he thought. The boy knew the great oak had provided shade for years, maybe even centuries, and it was time to give back. Children playing in the forest saw the boy and spread the word: all the boys and girls in the village started searching for poles. When the poles ran out they searched for sticks. Soon the great oak was sheltered from the sun. A girl raised her voice in song and the children joined in. Leaves quit falling as the great oak listened.

Sirens in Santa Cruz

Girls, blonde and delicious,

Storm like new season

From veranda

Over to the bar.

This foursome makes music

With micros waving

And stilettos

Tap-tapping the tiles.

The bartender

Arms them with margaritas.

Their mouths

Are filled with pearls.

NOTES ABOVE WATER

Men play the background shy,

Not knowing how to converse

With sudden goddesses.

The girls whisper and giggle

About a George Clooney look-alike

Alone at the end of the bar.

Tongues pass through scarlet lips

To lick the salt from glasses.

Voice

I HATE my voice. But I didn't use to. In third grade I sang a mean mezzo-soprano in the boys choir. Girls fell in love with me. In fifth grade I won the talent show for my high-pitched recital of "Trees" by Joyce Kilmer. "Angelic," said the nun.

But my voice didn't advance, I mean, it didn't turn masculine. Women who hear me today swear I'm gay. Telemarketers call me "Ma'am." My girlfriend says not to worry but I'm sure her friends think she's shacked up with a bi, at best. It doesn't help that I'm an artist. I watch football and drink beer on weekends, thinking maybe that will shift me to tenor. It hasn't. I lower my voice if I pick up the phone and stick to monosyllables and grunts. Occasionally I get a "Hello, Sir." When that happens it makes my day.

If my girlfriend ever leaves me I think I'll become a monk. Aren't they sworn to silence? I'd be great in Old Testament days, when they would cut off your tongue for blasphemy. I'd curse God left and right until a priest's dagger sawed away, banishing my voice to the Lake of Fire.

SoCal Storm

The ground exceeds saturation.

Owners drain backyard pools

With rented pumps and hoses.

Dogs growl the raindrops.

Waterspouts sighted off Newport.

Coastal roofs prepare for their beating.

Here's the 3rd storm in a series of 4.

Huntington's tornado lifted a houseboat.

Wind roars at the windows.

The screens rattle.

Neighborhood chimes ring like xylophones.

Palms and bamboo flutter most—

Leaves excite and shout

Like teenagers at a car wash.

Pines and oaks are mostly stoic;

Arms sway but spines remain

As true as iron.

Disneyland and Knotts threaten to close.

A plastic cup skids over asphalt.

Cats hunker down on blankets.

The mailman delivers mail fast,

Speeds the block like a demon.

The ice cream truck's on hiatus.

It's a good day for delivery pizza.

Sparrows dance in weeds and grass,

Rescue most of the drowning.

Poolside at the Santa Fe Hilton

Indigo clouds expand then contract,

Perform a kabuki act

Above the frigid pool.

Lightning strikes register in Taos

And Colorado ghost towns.

Morning hail butchered the cottonwoods,

Dented my hybrid rental.

The sun plays hide and seek in the mercurial sky.

The Jacuzzi's roped off with yellow ribbon.

Limp water refuses to bubble.

Two men, foreheads goggled,

Huddle penis deep in the shallows.

"Marco," says one of the men.

"Polo," giggles the other.

A girl with turquoise cowboy hat

Backgammons her boyfriend on lounge chairs.

She surveys the pool, bored by his attention.

A raindrop strikes me between the eyes.

Clouds fuse to become faces.

The one over the Sangre de Cristos

Sports Dadio's profile.

I enter the water, wade west

Until septuagenarian breasts sink into blue.

A breeze corrugates the surface.

The sun slips behind a cloud.

"Yes, yes, yes," the backgammon girl says,

Thrusts golden arms into the sky.

Shadows bleed east over apricot flagstone.

At the Coffee House

SHE STANDS BESIDE THE DOORWAY watching him wait in line with his old college buddy. "Tall Americano," he orders. He wears the aqua shorts she picked out to show off his butt and a dobby hat to hide the salt in his hair. There are girls behind him, coeds really, and he starts flirting. A blonde with hair past her waist giggles at something he says. The old college buddy joins in and it becomes a party. So many smiles, so much flashing of teeth.

She steps back into twilight. She doesn't want coffee or cheesecake. It's something they do as a couple but the old college buddy makes her feel like a third wheel. She sits at a brick fire pit on the patio. The flames are orange and green. She spots him through glass—he clutches a venti-sized cup and performs exaggerated gestures like a silent movie star. The blonde is smiling. She hears the old college buddy's machinegun laugh. She kicks off her slippers. She swings bare feet up on brick, toes reaching for fire.

View from the 5th Floor

The hospice light is flawless.

The steel in my room gleams.

Gold embraces the linoleum.

Outside, butterflies tease the bougainvillea

With tongues.

The eastern hills are green.

Crows fly by without faces.

A red hawk perched on a fence

Devours a pigeon.

The wind carries the smell of blood

Through my screen.

Pines have fallen from last night's storm—

They lie helpless in the next lot,

Roots burning in the sun.

Trees have joined me on the horizontal,

A level where the body

Can be easily poked and prodded.

This place breeds vertical nurses,

Transfusions, doctors whispering in doorways.

A white coat photographs me

Nude on my canvas.

I am a shutterbug's delight,

A deconstructing subject.

The lens blinks my mortality.

Message from a Vet

I limp ankle bandages

Across the spongy carpet.

TV advertises flags, dead Iraqis.

The President's smiling

At his podium. He orders

Fear, dining out, continental travel.

My orange cat

Snores on his saffron pillow.

Ankles are strange joints—

They attach the body

To its walking roots.

Ligaments move back and forth

Like slaves rowing

A Roman galleon.

My ligaments rebel

Against the patriarchal empire.

Notes from Crater Lake

October moon breaks the caldera.

Ancient light summons the ghosts.

Spirit warriors meet on the ridge.

A deer's cry sharpens the stars.

Ancient light summons the ghosts.

Scent of onion shrub and pine.

A deer's cry sharpens the stars.

Warriors march Crater Rim Road.

Scent of onion shrub and pine.

The hemlock cones rattle.

Warriors march Crater Rim Road.

The lake becomes sky.

An owl circles Danger Bay.

Spirit warriors meet on the ridge.

Llao's Fingers weave through the depths.

October moon breaks the caldera.

Moon

The moon's a bowl tonight

Collecting dreams over the sea.

When I was a boy

It followed me through eucalyptus.

I got a telescope for Christmas,

Studied the moon like Galileo.

You'll never see the dark side,

Big Brother said.

I scoured the Sea of Tranquility

For astronauts, imagined

The Stars & Stripes

Fluttering in the lunar breeze.

Now I keep telescope eyes

To the ground

Looking for change.

I pretend shines from Heaven

Are over-active streetlights.

The moon's become distant,

Like a friend dumped off

At a bus stop

On a country road

Lost and long forgotten.

30 Years Between Letters

Words from an old flame

Sunrise the past

The time of immortality

When the future

Was not reduced

But expansive as ocean

At sunset

Where you embraced

In a green flash

You would never see again

And believed in fire

Beyond the sea of shadows.

Lost Love Revisited

YOU FIND A MINSTREL version of Bashful the autumn after we graduate and hide in Ashland working Shakespeare trying to make babies to forget me while snow falls as I stumble in a world of reunion fantasies, drugs, and look-alike sex until years kill dreams and I fall for someone singing "Purple Rain" on a sunny day in October.

How Disney our lives would have been with me writing and you drawing castles with puppy-eyed dragons and royals necking on parapet balconies.

We meet in a parallel universe where you recognize me at graduation as Prince Charming and park your vintage MG outside my home and sneak through the twilight window to join me on a big round bed with satin sheets and we kiss so deep our souls fuck and I play the prince while you bounce between Snow White and Cinderella feeling me slip off your bra as our bodies throb on sheets wet with moon.

The Last Aztec Mocha

SHE ANNOUNCES to baristas and locals at the coffee bar that this will be her last Aztec Mocha for a year because she's off to Hanalei Bay tomorrow morning. There's an avalanche of hugs and tears. She wants to be missed. And she will be missed for her purchases and tapping out of caffeine-inspired monologues on the chocolate floor.

There will be no applause when she returns in twelve months. No one will admire her strings of *puka* shells, sniff her *pikake* perfume, or ask if Kauai's waters are warm. The familiars will have moved on to new hangouts and jobs as she waits for her first Aztec Mocha in a bar filled with strangers.

Book 3

Unholy

Unions

Marriage

She loves him,

but in a different way.

She feels it's more

brother and sister

than husband and wife.

Their marriage? Unexpected.

They were cubicle chums,

worker bees

relegated to anonymity

in the corporate honeycomb.

Tealeaf and palm readers

said she'd marry

a man her father's age.

She touches herself

under the sheets

to make sure she's real,

that her life is more

than playing invisible.

A snore from deep in his chest

sounds his dream.

Snacking with Mahmoud

MAHMOUD SLAMS the door on Tehran. His face is gaunt and he's wearing a tattered tuxedo. A pistol's tucked in his cummerbund. "Asalama alaikum," I say and he winces. He reaches into a bowl perched on my dresser. I don't want to tell him it's cat food. "Difficult to find much during the occupation," he admits, chewing. My cat Dodo comes in—she leaps up on the dresser and nudges Mahmoud's hand away with her head. Mahmoud holds up a kibble and examines it. "What's in here cats like?" "Fish," I say, "only dried fish." Mahmoud nods. He opens the door and pulls out his pistol. "Do you brush the cat's teeth?" he asks. "Sometimes," I go. "Americans," he spits, "treat pets better than humans." I watch Mahmoud disappear into a cloud of dust swirling in the sunset.

Recluse

KID SISTER WANTS to hide out. "Hide out from what?" I ask. "Life," she answers. I'm not sure what brought this on, although I suspect it has something to do with Dadio beating us. He beat me mostly, but he beat her too because she had to live through my screams. She got so good at disappearing I figured she'd become the next David Copperfield. She's deadly serious about moving to either the German countryside or a remote island inhabited by flightless birds. She thinks it's brave to run but I feel she's being a coward. I scare her when I say no husband and no children mean dying alone in Bavaria or in the middle of the Pacific. I mention the option of marriage, since it requires semi-seclusion behind walls and doors. "Making babies in the dark," I smile. "Ew, sick," she mutters, "I hate bald, gurgling creatures." She recoils imagining sharing a house with a man. "I suppose he expects me to cook," she groans. I suggest wedding a chef or someone who frequents the farmer's market. "Will he like pasta?" she asks. "Sure," I go, "most guys love Italian." She lightens up after I tell her he'll be busy working and she'll be by herself most of the day. I remind her that, if she does end up with a chef, he'll be at the restaurant all night and will snooze away the sunshine hours. "Rarely cross paths," I whisper. "I suppose you're right," she admits, "as long as this dude respects my privacy." She says she has a good recipe for salmon and may bake every two weeks, that is, if he doesn't expect her to answer the door and pretends she's a ghost holidays and weekends.

Barren

Deceased cats and dogs

Are immortalized

In snaps on the fridge.

There was a pig too

And a vagabond tortoise.

Outdoor birds are easy:

We never see them die.

A revolving door of pets,

Hill dotted with plots,

Crosses, roses showing

Browning petals.

A baby's cry

From the hilltop

Pierces the woman

In bed beside me

Deeper than cock.

Confessions of a Retiree at Christmas

in memory of Jack Micheline

Funny how skin folds in on itself,

A canvas limp over muscle and bone.

My wedding band's stuck

Behind the second knuckle.

I nibble trail mix

As my Greyhound groans toward Vegas.

Tumbleweeds roll through the crosswalks.

Venus appears over a mesa.

We enter the Land of Driveways:

Children barefoot the asphalt

Watching Dadio string lights

Under the eave of their roof.

Mother's at the door hanging a wreath.

I weep behind a moonlit window

While stars dance the Zodiac sky.

Night Marchers

Silhouettes appear

In moonlight,

An army of ghosts

Bound by sorrow.

They march the shore

Looking for something

They lost, or someone

Who lost them

When they were dreams

Spilling over the sand.

To a Friend at the Ben Hur Apartments

A CATARACT SKY on Hyde. Something flies by—an albatross or a plane. You're up on the 6th floor where the bed bugs live. I like Ben Hur's cobalt canopy. A boy in jeans enters the shade, searches the list of dwellers. Salt greens your buzzer. Don't miss his shy ring boiling water for Earl Grey.

I have seen your bvds tumble dry at Dair's Speedy Wash. You buy cognac at Serve Well Market. Cigars at Mini Smoke Shoppe. Your voice drags Sunday mornings, when we sip espresso at breeze window watching our city shrink to a village. Smell ocean? Below us, the escape ladder slants 60 degrees. Traffic's one way. A loose dog pisses a hydrant.

Oceanside Beach

Pink and yellow umbrellas

Frost the foggy sand.

Surfers in wetsuits

Bob like apples

In a green-gray stew.

Sails fatten with wind.

Delicious bikinis patrol the strand.

The Beach Boys croon from a bungalow.

Two girls for every boy,

A woman for every man.

Toddlers toy with plastic shovels

While margaritas are sipped

From cans. The celebration goes on for miles.

The marine layer gets assaulted

By the noonish sun—

Waves will turn jade

In less than an hour.

When I was younger

The beach seemed warmer.

Sir, have you seen my wife?

Legs churning north in aqua shorts?

Surging foam picks up clumps of kelp,

Tumbleweeds them over the sand.

Checkered black and yellow flags

Warn of currents and tragic undertows.

Sun ignites our faces—

We're exposed

Like drunks at a bar ready to close.

Poem for a Poet

These days I find blood

In strange places,

Drops falling like rain

Staining the carpet.

I remember the razor dragging,

Unzipping me from myself.

Why do I plant

The arms and legs of dolls

In the earth

Of the redwood planter?

It amuses you.

I know.

Am I planting myself?

My only pictures of you

Are on the flaps of books.

You search for women

To belong to

When you know, deep down,

You belong to me

Or at least the part of me

That makes you hunger

For more bloody morsels.

Oceanfront Condo

The wind hurls

A barrage of clouds

Into the palms.

We are between seasons

On a shore

Swollen with kelp.

I am a bald man

Lying in bed

Waiting for rain.

I play Solitaire

With tarot cards

Pecking at love.

Yesterday, a kidney stone.

Today arthritis.

Bell's palsy delivers

Permanent damage.

I radiate my brain

I-Phoning the Church.

The optimistic priest

Sprinkles Holy Water

On dead dandelions.

Disney Postcard at Christmas

VOICI PERFECTION! Such happy cheeks, this quartet posing outside Blue Ribbon Bakery on Main Street. See how Daddy and Mommy frame their little angels? The angels flank Minnie Mouse. I remember when Mommy had an affair with a co-worker and Daddy visited a strip joint to pout.

I like Daddy's panama hat. His angels have hats too. The girl angel clutches a vinyl handbag. The boy angel has palms pressed, as if praying. Mommy wears a muumuu and a checkered bow in her hair. Daddy and Mommy look stiff, as if pretending to be walls.

I appreciate the exclamation points in the message, and the admission (I'm sure that's Mommy's cursive) their photo was snapped during a heat wave in August. You'd never know it wasn't December, judging by the joyful eyes, jolly smiles, and teeth bright as holiday snow.

At Buccaneer Park

Palms sway like drunks

Along the Oceanside boardwalk.

Summer's gone.

Windows at Sam's Snack Shop

Are boarded up.

Two boys tug of war

A green boogie board.

A crow rips into a bag

In the beer bottle trash.

A girl moans

Inside a rocking van.

Smell blood on the wind?

Her cry is thirteen,

Fourteen tops.

A man yanks his collared golden

Down to the sand.

I could die on a day like this,

Sunny wind at 3 pm

On a Sunday losing at halftime

A gun held to my head.

Leg of Jen

MY PARENTS are having my sister's leg for dinner. June Spoon, my mother, asks if I'm hungry and I tell her no, that I just pigged out at McDonald's. Dadio scolds me for filling up on junk food. "No room in the inn?" June Spoon jokes. Dadio lips smack on a hunk of hindquarter. "Succulent," he hums, "you don't know what you're missing." Funny, he never said that when my calf was the main course for Easter two years ago.

I hobble up the hall. I find Jen in her room, in bed under the sheets. It smells like urine and blood. My sister tells me she's lost her appetite and wouldn't eat herself anyway no matter how good our parents say she tastes. She says they took both legs, that her left's out in the freezer. I distract myself by checking out Bob, her four-foot boa, which she keeps in a glass terrarium propped on her chest of drawers. Bob looks much smaller coiled on his river stones.

"How will you get around, Jen?" I ask. "I'll manage," she answers, "don't you?" I tell her yes. Then I realize why she's under the sheets—she's hiding her body. I'd forgotten Dadio took an arm on Independence Day. But she adapted like a champ to an artificial one with robotic features clad in flesh-colored silicone. Still, it's too bad Jen's only got one limb. "Never let them get the other arm," I caution. "Oh, no," she goes, "they're saving that for Christmas." Jen gazes at the terrarium. She tells me she'll learn how to slither by studying Bob, whenever he hunts mice in his glass cage. She promises to be as mobile as Bob, maybe even better, as she slithers toward dinner down the hall.

Son of Crab

I AM A SICK MAN lying on a twin bed listening to rain. I have learned cold showers in a solar house inhabited by crabs. Dadio crab sits in a wheelchair clicking his remote. June Spoon crab devours mahi-mahi out of a doggie bag. I have the maid's room. The maid left years ago. The crabs go to bed at midnight, him in his hospital bed with a view of the red ti garden, her in the king they once shared. They would claw one another when the salmon curtains were drawn. Now they scuttle through the house searching for water, entertainment, dead things to eat. Outside, rain floods the street. My skin hardens as I write.

Book 4
Final Act in Paris

Outside the Boulangerie

Man on foot with bike shoes

Reminds me of a woman

In bright heels

Negotiating cobblestones.

I remember mother

Walking the plank

Down the hall,

Stilettos clicking toward

The master bedroom.

There were bills

Owed to the master,

Bills paid in flesh

After the curtains were drawn,

The AC fired up,

And the door locked.

The man with bike shoes

Wobbles a path

Strewn with white petals.

My mother wept

When the door swung open

And the AC quit blowing.

The aroma of baking bread

Drifts from the boulangerie.

Bike man wolfs a croissant.

Mothers stroller by

Discussing the weights

Of their babies.

Trip and Fall

I may trip and fall

Through these glass shower doors,

Blood and shards everywhere.

Two of the shards

Bounce into the toilet.

A third finds the sink.

The drain washes

More and more of me away

Under the spurting shower.

I will survive stitches

And see a woman

Standing in the doorway,

Hands on swollen hips.

She is my woman, I think.

Her eyes become paths

To the dangerous present.

A baby cries in her womb.

I hunger from losing blood.

She slices a hunk of moon,

Serves it on a blue plate

Soon after midnight.

Ring Finger

A MAN FILMS HIS WIFE descending their outdoor staircase. She's flattered because she's always wanted to be a model. The steps creak. She thinks he resembles a dwarf aiming up from the driveway. She wishes she'd married another man. The dwarf tells her to return to the top when she's halfway down because he needs to reset her lighting. She spins around. The steps seem taller and are more difficult to climb. Her ring finger throbs at the joint.

5 a.m. on a Work Day

Venus near zenith.

Birds nonexistent.

Trees missing their leaves.

Engines whisper my street.

Birds nonexistent.

Cats avoid glass.

Engines whisper my street.

Roof slants like a ladder.

Cats avoid glass.

Dogs bark a riot.

Roof slants like a ladder.

House vents are gills.

Streetlights extinguish.

Trees missing their leaves.

Gray clouds the horizon.

Venus near zenith.

The Secret World of Men

You lost me

As a friend

When you farted

In the neighboring urinal

At the Mandarin House

Without an apology

On my birthday

When I picked up

The check.

Did I find you

Blowing wind

Uncouth? Disrespectful?

Or was I realizing

You were human

After all, that you

Let secrets escape

In public places

On special occasions

With hardly

A care in the world.

At Lofty Coffee, Encinitas

A blonde barista

In a felt fedora

Dreams in the steam

Off the espresso machine.

Sneakers and sandals

Slap the chocolate floor.

The sun slants in

Through louvers. Behind glass,

A pink beach cruiser rusts

At bars, spokes, and basket.

Girls toy with phones

Beside the hydrant.

A red Mustang pulls over

On the corner of A Street

And Coast Highway.

The barista tongs a brownie.

Moon River Interlude

June Spoon is my mother.

She laughs at my artistic endeavors.

A wart clings to her nose.

She's a failed cabaret singer.

She laughs at my artistic endeavors.

I helped get her cd on the internet.

She's a failed cabaret singer.

She sings "Moon River" with passion.

I helped get her cd on the internet.

June Spoon spread her legs for a brute.

She sings "Moon River" with passion.

She fell at my sister's wedding.

She says I'm no longer her son.

A wart clings to her nose.

Making art is always a struggle.

June Spoon is my mother.

Laws of Attraction

SHE LOVED HIM because he worshipped her. Her style of love operated more out of loyalty than attraction, the way an owner is loyal to a dog that fawns and slobbers. Sex with him was tolerable. It did excite her that he'd abandoned his wife and three children to be with her. She used his worship as a platform to support her movie star ambitions, even though she was over forty and had never been on film except uncredited roles as waitresses, hookers, and faces in the mob. She ached to be famous. He knew her passion and gave her foot rubs whenever she felt blue. She left him for an actor half her age she swore was the second coming of Tom Cruise.

The Pain-Body

for Eckhart Tolle

I FLOP IN BED, placing a fiver over my heart. I want to lure the pain-body to the surface to see what's shaping my thoughts. I'm guessing it resembles a pulsating blob of tar. I can't get angry waiting. I must remain in a trance to draw the creature out. I forget childhood beatings. I ignore my divorce. The future? Meaningless.

My bowels pop. There's a stabbing in my tailbone and a tug at the penis. Something claws from spine to liver and swings the rib cage. I feel teeth gnawing through my heart. I hide the bill under a pillow. A phantom with a platinum bouffant and red lipstick erupts from my chest, teeth flashing gold. "Gimme that money," demands Mummy, who died a year ago last June.

Pain Pills

I can swallow two bottles of pills

To burst my heart in peace.

Who cares about passing?

They say there's no pain

In the other world,

If I'm brave enough

To leap off Earth's edge.

It's easy flying my carcass

Through thin air

When the bottles are empty

And refill chances

Have been cancelled.

Butchering Day

Sever my arthritic feet,

Toss them to coyotes

Hunting in packs

In the Mojave.

Fresh meat in pain

Is still fresh meat.

Let them taste

Poetry in my blood.

Watch them gnaw

Ankles, tendons, toes.

Hear them howl

When I tumble

Into their bellies

Under the blue moon

Of butchering day.

Keeping the Darkness Out

How fast the sun arrives

And disappears, its arc

Belonging to yesterday

As whiskey and cigarettes

Future forward.

The night turns to lust

To keep the darkness out.

We are addicted to

The warmth of bodies

Genuflecting bedposts,

Praying we survive

The heat of battle

Until light brings

The cold tomorrow.

Ice Mother

June Spoon is dead to me.

She's still alive,

But my love for her

Has evaporated

Like rain on hot sidewalk.

Your mother will always

Be your best friend,

Dadio promised.

That promise was a lie.

He knew she was

Made of ice,

Cold to the touch

Eyes frigid in photos.

She hates me

For becoming the beloved

Of another woman.

She hates me

For loving and being loved.

The last thread of hope

Has been severed.

Carrots on Snow

A FLAME has been extinguished in mother, not the fire of life but that spark wanting independence. She displays a certain resignation, one that causes her face to droop as if melting. Her body sags in the chair. The dining table's cluttered with magazines, keys, unopened credit card statements and utility bills, newspapers, and expired coupons from Whole Foods. She nods solemnly when I suggest she consider a live-in to help prepare meals and keep things tidy. "You could be like roommates," I smile, "and, best of all, she could drive you everywhere." "Driving Miss Lonely," she smirks, getting up. She weaves her way through a gauntlet of boxes marked for recycling, crates of junk mail, and plastic bins filled with ornaments. She shuffles past the Christmas tree and falls into the loveseat beside the window. She studies the rabbits. They're gnawing the carrots she stacked on the snow at dawn.

Final Act in Paris

Room smells of pinot and sex.

The human morning bangs itself.

Last night was first touch.

Rue Saint-Martin is a rage of wheels.

The human morning bangs itself.

Dreams break the lights.

Rue Saint-Martin is a rage of wheels.

White petals melt over bricks.

Dreams break the lights.

Survival leaks to tragic.

White petals melt over bricks.

Warriors erupt from the carpet.

Tulips bloom red in a vase.

Last night was first touch.

Girl becomes her mother at dawn.

Room smells of pinot and sex.

Book 5
Notes
Above
Water

Life Extension

With modern medicine, isn't all life artificial?

Wonder drugs make us artifacts, might someday

Preserve us longer than Methuselah, the antediluvian.

Walt Disney's still alive in a cryogenic sense,

His skin as blue as Matterhorn snow. It's a wonder

 I survived babyhood after three convulsions,

Thank god Mrs.Tamura held down my tongue with a

Spoon. Lives keep extending, making postwar babies

The envy of their prewar parents. What about pets?

That cat down the street isn't breathing the way he did

Last week. Must be his diet. Some owners give their

Dogs and cats Life Extension, either in powder or tablets.

After powder, Grandma's Chihuahua wants to be bounced on

My knee like a baby. My vet says animal longevity can't be

Predicted. He's right, especially when you consider the

Omnipresent threat of traffic. In the human world,

Orchestra conductors live the longest—something about

Commanding with hands, making faces, waving a wand

In front of trained musicians. I doubt train conductors live

As long, although their approach whistle might resemble

A note blown from an archangel's trumpet. My uncle wanted

Taps played over his grave. Will I be buried with

Cuff links polished? Gold watch strapped to my wrist?

Saint Michael on a swimmer's chain around my neck?

A classmate I once loved keeps getting posthumous

Awards in my quarterly bulletin, this one for

Lifetime Achievement. It's as if she never really left.

Our lives keep overlapping in *Alumni Notes*, even though

In high school we hardly touched. Sometimes I break out

The tarot deck, work it like a Geiger counter—

Detecting spiritual fallout, measuring ethereal

Particles, interpreting her half-life, trying to kiss a ghost.

Friedrich Speaks

The apocalypse has been cancelled.

There will be no stench of death

Wafting over the plains.

Wildflowers will still bloom.

Forget a blaring of trumpets

Announcing the end of days.

It will be dark soon.

Last kisses? Nonexistent.

I will be planted Catholic

In a plot on a green lawn

With a view of the sea.

I will be remembered

As an obstacle to the blade

Of the lawnmower man.

Sparrows dance my headstone.

View from the Burbs

Wine bodies gather in driveways.

Voices carry message of babies.

Flesh creators stroller by twins.

Motor coaches stinking of diesel.

Voices carry message of babies.

Men chainsaw weeds.

Motor coaches stinking of diesel.

Widow squirts walkway lamps.

Men chainsaw weeds.

Gardens force birth before taps.

Widow squirts walkway lamps.

Trash and recyclables on Fridays.

Girl sucks a hula-hoop.

Flesh creators stroller by twins.

SUVs wrinkle the asphalt.

Wine bodies gather in driveways.

Requiem for a Pool Man

I nod half-smiles

In waiting rooms,

Breathing the stink

Of latex gloves

And rubbing alcohol,

Waiting for nurses to call.

I was the changer of tides,

The boy throwing stones

Into the sea

To send surf raging

Toward distant shores.

Now I clean pools

In Trump Tower shadows,

Imagining a lost daughter

Spreading blankets

Over my grave.

The Young Novelist from Manila

The young novelist from Manila

Mingles with writers, poets, professors

In the Fung Shui Room

At the Marco Polo Hotel, Hong Kong.

"Wot's yo' novel about?" a woman asks.

"It's a murder mystery," he answers, "set in Quezon City."

The young novelist wears shiny blue Versace jeans

And believes his scarf looks best

Swirled twice around the neck, then stuffed

Inside the lapels of his steel-gray jacket.

Dr. Fong, awards coordinator, pats him on the shoulder.

"Smaht casual," compliments Fong.

"A mock cravat," the young novelist jokes.

700 miles southeast in the Philippines,

The young novelist's father

Hides with 300 henchmen

In an Ampatuan mangrove, Maguindanao Province.

They've blocked the dirt road with bulldozers.

The father hears engines.

Dito dumating sila, he warns.

The young novelist keeps secrets well:

The $100,000/year trust, an all-expense paid

Romp through the MFA Program at NYU,

Steady cocaine, a Trump Towers penthouse,

The slew of ghost writers and editors-for-hire,

Being a *paminta*,

And his Director-General father who habitually

Plunders the Youth Education Fund

At the Department of Labor.

Syota, a model-thin blonde calls from the foyer, *mahal kita!*

The young novelist's lover

Has just arrived from Montreal—

She hugs the young novelist, kisses him

Hard on the lips. He kisses softly back.

She wears matching Versace jeans,

A red blouse, gold heels,

And answers to "Eleanore."

The young novelist prefers old-fashioned names,

Just like his father.

700 miles southeast in the Philippines,

Men charge out of the mangrove

And ambush a convoy of political rivals.

57 men and women kneel on the zoysia grass

Surrounded by machetes, guns, automatic rifles.

End loaders scrape open the earth

Behind the mangrove.

Hindi ako sa kanila, a woman begs.

Subalit ikaw ay isang saksi, the father answers.

The young novelist bites a cookie,

Washes it down with jasmine tea.

He rests his left hand

Inside his jacket, pretends to be Napoleon.

Lumpia, pork adobo, and pansensia

Are being served in the Feng Shui Room

In honor of his homeland.

He remembers the stink of cabbage,

The vulgar smells of vinegar and fish sauce

Rising from the family kitchen.

Once he choked down dog pot with his father

In a Baguio back alley.

Malapit na kami ay tumahol, his father had kidded.

700 miles southeast in the Philippines,

The women are raped, the men beheaded.

After the raping, the women are beheaded too.

"It is for the best," the father thinks,

Proud his son has defeated

So many important writers.

He orders the bodies dragged over the zoysia

To a big shallow grave.

Heads follow the bodies—they roll like leaky coconuts

And get wedged between arms and legs.

The young novelist stands at the podium

Stroking his jaw as the cameras flash.

A white piano plays Satie's *Gymnopédies*.

The reporter from Asia TV Limited

Videotapes beside the doorway.

The music fades.

"I am humbled by your award," begins the young novelist.

Eleanore flashes the thumbs up.

Dr. Fong beams in the front row.

700 miles southeast in the Philippines,

The father puffs a La Flor de Isabela cigar.

He wishes he could be with his boy.

Takip sa libingan na may sanga ng bakawan, he tells his men.

He is comforted by the thought

His son will do just fine without him

Because everything the young novelist knows

He learned from his father.

Notes:

dito dumating sila: here they come

paminta: closet gay

syota: sweetheart

mahal kita: I love you

hindi ako sa kanila: I am not with them

subalit ikaw ay isang saksi: but you are a witness

dog pot: dog prepared as a stew and served in a clay pot

malapit na kami ay tumahol: soon we will bark

takip sa libingan na may sanga ng bakawan: cover the grave with mangrove branches

The Monster in the House

The hate in him keeps him alive.

As a child he was studious and loved challenges.

Sucking marrow from bone became his specialty.

He beats the oldest to break the others.

As a child he was studious and loved challenges.

Wife retreats to kitchen during the tortures.

He beats the oldest to break the others.

He's a lawyer feasting on children.

Wife retreats to kitchen during the tortures.

Lying upsets him most because he's a liar.

He's a lawyer feasting on children.

Neighbors pretend to hear and see nothing.

He wants you to fear him.

Sucking marrow from bone became his specialty.

His mother made her mother raise him.

The hate in him keeps him alive.

On Finding a Lost Friend

When you lose touch with a friend

And don't speak for 35 years

That first call

Feels like a job interview

And you pray your friend

Hasn't forgotten what you remember.

When you talk

The years vanish

And you're back in your dorm

Drinking beer and talking crushes

As the first snow falls.

The Girl With the Green Violin

She is the band to me,

A splash of blonde on brown bangs,

Hair spilling to shoulders,

Small hand gliding bow over strings.

She stands under lights

At the edge of the stage

Firing song through a pub

Smelling of whiskey and stout.

Wall to wall men stand spellbound.

Fingers stroke the violin's neck.

She is an angel in denim

And mint sweater

Coaxing demons from a fiddle

Glowing Celtic emerald.

She summons the ghosts.

She finds the boy in me—

I am a man buried in debt

Bewitched back to the surface

By strings. I ache to jig her

Across the beer-stained floor

Through double doors

Until my skin burns

With blood moon.

I want a stone cottage

Overlooking the sea,

Sheep grazing my rise,

And the girl with the green violin

Playing forever beside me.

Advice for a Poet Abroad

Stay horizontal that first week.

Head vertical when

Your shadow joins

Another on the wall.

Scribble dreams on leaves

The texture of parchment.

Drop leaves off bridges

Into currents swirling north.

North is where the mountains are.

Place coins in outstretched palms.

Savor the smells of cheeses,

Woody incense, farmer's markets.

Avoid phoning home.

Drape guilt and sorrow

Off street lamps

Like garlands of garlic.

Drink cheap wine

Splashing from bars.

Contemplate cobblestones:

Ghosts whisper through cracks.

Trump Tower Waikiki

Concierge says eight floors up.

Upgrade earns a couch.

Marble bathroom vacuous.

Bikinis on a veranda.

Upgrade earns a couch.

Shadows on bone-white plates.

Bikinis on a veranda.

Boy stones an indigo sea.

Shadows on bone-white plates.

Clouds bandage the sun.

Boy stones an indigo sea.

Cup loads bleach the pool.

Tiki torches flash at dusk.

Marble bathroom vacuous.

Rubber plumerias in gift shop.

Concierge says eight floors up.

House With Dragon Trees

THE SUN WARMS this morning before Easter, paralyzing cats in windows. "Pop Goes the Weasel" plays. Tiny feet chatter chasing an ice cream truck. There was a neighborhood below the volcano. I see a house with dragon trees, a net above the garage, backyard swings.

I return to bed. Teary Eary, my plush dog, remembers. See the boy run on cuts legs. Hear a soprano howl as the belt sings. Smell the iron scent of blood. Teary's fur is worn from hugging and biting.

At twilight, I rise and float ghost-like over the driveway. The children are gone. Popsicle sticks lie in the gutter. I flip the mailbox lid to find a bomb inside—an Easter card from Daddy.

The Woman in the Black One Piece

She crosses legs on the lounge chair,

rests the book on her belly.

She smoothes lotion

over arms and shoulders.

Funny how skin learns

pink instead of copper.

Men sleep in Speedos

on the other side of the pool.

She knows she's invisible

even to the man wheeling

a canvas cart, stuffing it with towels.

She contemplates the pool—

her pain goes deeper

than twelve feet under the board.

Axes have swung at her soul.

No Lifeguard on Duty,

Swim at Your Own Risk.

She treats wounds

with fantasy and chocolate.

She hears newlyweds

giggling inside the Jacuzzi,

recalls the aftermath

of a quilt spread

beside the picnic river.

The morning of stained glass promises

she believed, she really believed.

She slips on her glasses

and arrives at a Tuscan villa.

An Italian with a mustache

parachutes into the heroine's life.

She studies a sky too blue,

too deep to be real.

The Neighbors

They motor coach into mountains and deserts.

His passion's the cleaning of windshields.

She's a stay-at-home mom with a Cockapoo.

He supports them selling online flowers.

His passion's the cleaning of windshields.

Their red-tiled roof should last forever.

He supports them selling online flowers.

He wants perimeter walls higher and higher.

Their red-tiled roof should last forever.

She clears her throat when gardening.

He wants perimeter walls higher and higher.

Their parked coach takes half-a-block.

She's never borrowed sugar, eggs, or butter.

She's a stay-at-home mom with a Cockapoo.

Their holiday parties are typically quiet.

They motor coach into mountains and deserts.

Notes Above Water

Captain says Hawaii's early,

To subtract six hours

Before landing.

I'm lousy adjusting hands

On Mondays when

The one I love

Lives in tomorrow's time zone.

Broken since four,

I have avoided babies

Fearing transformation

Into Dadio,

The maestro of martinis

And swinger of belts.

My wing rips open a cloud—

Below, hunks of lava

Float the violent teal.

They step to a place

Where the walls scream.

I study fragments

Searching for meaning

Along fingers of reef,

Jagged black shores,

Into the emerald shallows

That drown.

The Widow from Lake Bled

Selected Poems
Kirby Wright

Foreword by Joseph W. Bean

HONG KONG MAN

Selected Poems

KIRBY WRIGHT

BEFORE THE CITY

Selected Poems & Prose

KIRBY WRIGHT

FOREWORD BY DANIEL BOURNE

www.ingramcontent.com/pod-product-compliance
Lightning Source LLC
Chambersburg PA
CBHW051652040426
42446CB00009B/1093